Contents

Badger Publishing

New words:

mutants	disgusting
creatures	pollution
surrounded	extinction

Main characters:

Liam

Mr Marcus

Tig

Chapter 1
Mrs Spencer's Cat

Liam was walking by the canal with his dog. Most of his friends were on holiday.

Mr Marcus, from down the road, was fishing.

"Had any luck?" said Liam.

"Not a nibble," grumbled Mr Marcus.

Liam's dog trotted over.

"Hello, Tig! Have you been chasing cats?"

Liam laughed. Tig was frightened of cats!

"Look out for Mrs Spencer's cat will you?
It hasn't been home for days."

Liam said he would.

"See you, Mr Marcus. Hope they start
biting."

Liam carried on along the towpath.
The dog started to push through the
long grass at the side of the path.
"Here, Tig!" called Liam.
Tig didn't come. Liam went over to look.

A cloud of flies buzzed up from the spot.
It was Mrs Spencer's cat.
It's back half seemed to have
disappeared. It smelt disgusting.
Liam felt sick.

Liam called Mr Marcus.
"It's Mrs Spencer's cat all right!
I should say a fox has had it."

Liam noticed something odd.
"Look at the plants by the water.
They're all broken down."

Mr Marcus laughed.
"Must have been a crocodile that got
the cat! No, we mustn't laugh.
I'll go and tell Mrs Spencer."

He set off. Behind him, just above the
surface of the water, two eyes were
watching him.

Liam turned down a path through some trees. There was a small pond there.

It was amazing that anything lived in the pond. People dumped their rubbish in it.
Liam was worried about pollution.
The pond was full of frog spawn and he wanted to watch them turn into frogs.

By the side of the pond he saw a slimy mess. Liam guessed that someone had dumped a load of chemicals there.

"Come on, Tig," called Liam.

Angrily, he walked back to the canal.
Another favourite place ruined.

Behind him, hidden in the weeds, there
were more eyes watching.

Chapter 2

The Creature

Mr Marcus lived next to the canal.
Mrs Marcus was in the garden,
checking her plants.

Mr Marcus had decided not to go
fishing again. The fish weren't biting
today.

Mrs Marcus reached a patch of tall
plants at the bottom of the garden.
They're growing too big, she thought to
herself. I must cut them back.

Suddenly, out of the corner of her eye,
she saw something coming towards her.

She felt a sharp pain in her leg.
She cried out.

Mr Marcus heard her yelling.
He hurried to the door.

Mrs Marcus lay on the ground.
There was a dark shape next to her.
Mr Marcus grabbed a stick and rushed
down the garden path.

The creature was the size of a big dog.
It was green, with a round body.
It had a pointed head, with huge eyes
sticking out of the top of it.
Its mouth was full of savage-looking
teeth. Its feet had skin between the
toes, like a duck.
Its skin looked like wet leather.

Bravely, Mr Marcus rushed at it, hitting it with his stick.

The creature didn't like that. It turned back into the bushes, hopping along on its powerful back legs.

A short while later Liam heard an ambulance rushing past his house.

"Come on Tig," he said. "Let's see what's going on."

Chapter 3
Escaped

Liam was shocked when he saw that
the ambulance was outside the
Marcus's cottage. It drove off just as he
arrived.

Mrs Spencer was standing at her door.
"Poor Mrs Marcus has been attacked by
an animal. I bet it was the same one
that ate my Bobby."

"I'm sorry about your cat. How bad is
Mrs Marcus?"

"It took a big bite out of her leg.
Mr Marcus didn't know what it was.

Something that's escaped from one of those wildlife parks if you ask me."

Liam looked into the Marcus's garden. Suddenly, he noticed that Tig had disappeared.

"Tig, where are you?"

Tig rushed out of a hole in the fence. His tail was wagging. Liam looked at the hole. The grass was flat on both sides. He went over to the canal bank. Near it were traces of blood.

Liam took Tig home and set off to the hospital.

Mr Marcus was waiting in the casualty department. He was pleased to see Liam.
"Thanks for coming, lad."

"How is Mrs Marcus?"

"Not too bad. Luckily I was able to chase it off. She will need a lot of stitches though."

Mr Marcus told Liam about the strange animal.
"The doctors say it must have been a dog. I've never seen a dog like that! It was more like a huge frog."

Later that day Liam was busy on his computer.

He couldn't find the creature Mr Marcus had described.

He was thinking about something Mr Marcus had said. 'Like huge frogs...'

Liam set out for the canal.

Chapter 4

Surrounded!

There was nobody on the towpath. Liam headed for the pond. His idea was probably crazy, but he thought he would check it out.

The pond was the same. Nothing strange was happening. Liam turned to go.

One of the creatures was waiting for him on the path. Tig didn't like this creature at all. He barked angrily. Liam was glad he was on a lead. The frog creature took a leap towards them. Liam turned to run, dragging Tig along.

The creature looked savage, but it didn't move fast. It was too heavy to jump far. Liam tried to get round the pond. He could go through the trees and out to the road.

He stopped. Three more creatures were sliding out of the pond ahead of him! More of them were hopping through the trees...He was surrounded!

Tig was barking. He tugged and tugged on the lead. Suddenly, it snapped!

Tig rushed towards the frog creatures. One of them hopped forwards and opened its mouth, showing its sharp teeth.

Tig stopped being brave. He turned and ran off into the bushes.
"Come back, you stupid dog!" shouted Liam.

Tig took no notice. The barking died away. Liam wanted to run, but every path was blocked by the creatures.

They started to close in.

There was just one chance. Liam pulled himself up onto a branch of a tree.
The creatures snapped at him, but they couldn't reach him.

Liam was very wet and cold. No one ever came to the pond. He could be stuck there for days!

Two hours passed. Liam was shivering, even though it was Summer.

He closed his eyes for a minute.
How much longer?

Suddenly, he found himself falling out of the tree. He must have dozed off!

He could not stop himself. He hit the ground feet first. He felt a sharp pain as his ankle twisted under him. He lay there in agony. He couldn't move!

Where were the frog creatures?
If they found him there, he wouldn't have a chance!

At last Liam managed to struggle to his feet. His ankle didn't hurt quite so much. He guessed that he hadn't broken it. But where was Tig?

He found a broken branch. He used it as a walking stick. He hobbled back towards the canal. Something was sticking out onto the path.

Chapter 5

Two Eyes

It was the head of one of the frog
creatures.

Liam stood absolutely still.
The creature didn't move.
Bravely, Liam looked more closely.
Its mouth hung open. Green slime
oozed out...the creature was dead.

Liam got to Mr Marcus's house about the same time as Mr Marcus.

Liam was very upset about Tig.

"Maybe he'll be at home," said Mr Marcus.

Mr Marcus agreed that the pond must be where the creatures came from. He rang up the police and left a message. Then he walked Liam home.

The next day there was a knock on the door. A policeman stood there with a woman in an anorak. She was a government scientist. They wanted Liam to show them the pond.

At the pond, the scientist looked closely at the dead creature, then took samples from the pond.

"Why did it die?" asked Liam.

"Starvation. They had eaten every fish in the canal." said the scientist.

"What are these creatures?" asked the policeman.

"Mutants. There's a real mix of chemicals in this pond. It must have got into the water just as the tadpoles were forming."

"Are they all dead now?"

"Hope so. They were pretty dangerous beasts!"

Just then they heard a sound in the bushes. Perhaps one of them was left. If so, it was going to be very hungry! A shape shot out of the bushes and leapt at Liam.
It was Tig!

A little later, Liam set off home, all worries gone.

A hundred miles away, a big tanker was parked on a quiet road. A pipe led down to a stream. A smelly, brown liquid poured out of the pipe.

The driver knew he would make a lot of money out of this. He used this place before and no-one had found out.

Behind him, just above the surface of the water, two eyes were watching him.

- *In the story, frogs mutated (changed) into dangerous killers.*

Across the world, it isn't frogs that have changed, but a tiny fungus called Bd. This fungus used to be harmless to frogs, but now it is killing billions of them.

Why has the fungus changed?
Many scientists think that this has happened because of climate change.

How does it kill frogs?
Frogs take in water and important chemicals through their skin. The fungus makes it difficult for the chemicals to pass through. Without them, the frogs' hearts stop beating.

Is it only frogs that are affected?
No. The fungus is killing all sorts of amphibians, such as toads and newts.

How deadly is it?

In some places, such as South America and Australia, billions of amphibians have died, and whole species (types) have been wiped out.

Why do frogs matter?

Amphibians are an important part of the life of a pond or a stream. They are food for birds and animals. Scientists have found that tadpoles are important in stirring up mud, making the pond or stream a better place for tiny plants and animals to grow.

Can anything be done?

Scientists are finding ways to protect frogs kept in captivity. Protecting them in the wild is much more difficult, and time is running out.

Questions

Questions on the story:

- Why did Liam visit the pond?

- What did he see that made him angry?

- Read the description of the creature that attacked Mrs Marcus. Write down two facts that show it was like a frog.

- Why did the frog creatures die?

- Read the very end of the story again. What do you think happens next?

Questions on the frogs facing extinction section:

- What may have made the Bd fungus change?

- Why is it important to stop amphibians dying?

Midsummer Mutants

by David Orme

Illustrated by
Aleksandar Sotirovski

FULL FLIGHT
Schools Library and Information Services

Titles in Full Flight 7

Badger Publishing Limited
Suite G08, Business & Technology Centre
Bessemer Drive, Stevenage, Hertfordshire SG1 2DX
Telephone: 01438 791037   Fax: 01438 791036
www.badger-publishing.co.uk

Midsummer Mutants ISBN 978-1-84926-251-4

Text © David Orme 2010
Complete work © Badger Publishing Limited 2010

The right of David Orme to be identified as author
of this Work has been asserted by him in accordance
with the Copyright, Designs and Patents Act 1988.

Badger Publishing would like to thank Jonny Zucker
for his help in putting this series together.

Publisher: David Jamieson
Editor: Danny Pearson
Design: Fiona Grant
Illustration: Aleksandar Sotirovski
Printed and bound in China through Colorcraft Ltd, Hong Kong